AIRPLANES

by Darlene R. Stille

Content Adviser: Professor Sherry L. Field,
Department of Social Science Education, College of Education,
The University of Georgia
Reading Adviser: Dr. Linda D. Labbo,
Department of Reading Education, College of Education,
The University of Georgia

Compass Point Books
Minneapolis, Minnesota

Compass Point Books
3722 West 50th Street, #115
Minneapolis, MN 55410

Visit Compass Point Books on the Internet at *www.compasspointbooks.com* or e-mail your request to *custserv@compasspointbooks.com*

Photographs ©: Thomas D. Parker, cover, 6–7; Richard Hamilton Smith, 1; Richard Hansen, 4–5; Photo Network/David Vinyard, 8–9; Photo Network/Jian Chen, 10–11; William B. Folsom, 12–13, 21; Visuals Unlimited/Arthur Morris, 14–15; Gary W. Carter/Visuals Unlimited, 16–17; Hulton Getty/Archive Photos, 18, 20; Unicorn Stock Photos/Bernard Hehl, 22; Photo Network/Ted Schmoll, 23; Reuters/HO/Archive Photos, 24–25; Unicorn Stock Photos/Jean Higgins, 26.

Editors: E. Russell Primm and Emily J. Dolbear
Photo Researcher: Svetlana Zhurkina
Photo Selector: Melissa Voda
Designer: Melissa Voda

Library of Congress Cataloging-in-Publication Data
Stille, Darlene R.
   Airplanes / by Darlene R. Stille.
      p. cm. — (Transportation)
   Includes bibliographical references and index.
   ISBN 0-7565-0146-6 (library binding)
      1. Airplanes—Juvenile literature. [1. Airplanes.] I. Title.
   TL547 .S83 2001
   629.133'34—dc21 2001001431

Table of Contents

Let's Ride in an Airplane

A big plane comes in for a landing. You can see its wings and wheels and bright lights. It is heading for the airport. You are heading for the airport too. Planes take off and land at airports.

You are going on an airplane trip. First, you go to the check-in counter. You give the ticket agent your suitcase. He or she gives you a boarding pass. Now you can board the plane.

It's a Jet

tail

wing

body

jet engines

nose

Your plane is a big jet plane. It has two wings. It has two jet engines on each wing. The wings and the engines make an airplane fly.

The front part of the plane is called the nose. The middle part is called the body. The back part has a tail that sticks up in the air.

All the seats are in the body section. Your plane has more than 100 seats. Jumbo jets have more than 400 seats!

Meet the Pilot

The pilot flies the plane. The pilot sits up front in the **cockpit.** The cockpit is full of dials, switches, buttons, levers, and pedals. The pilot uses them to make the plane go up and down. He or she also uses them to turn right and left, and to stop and go. A copilot helps the pilot fly the plane. Sometimes a **flight engineer** also helps fly the plane.

Out on the Runway

Fasten your seatbelt. The plane is ready to go. The doors shut. The plane moves away from the gate. It is going to the runway.

The runway is a long paved strip, like a wide road. Planes take off and land on a runway. Your plane goes down a taxi-way to get to the runway. Many planes are waiting to take off. Look out the window at the different kinds of planes.

Propeller Planes

Some planes have **propeller** engines instead of jet engines. Propeller planes cannot fly as fast as jet planes.

Some small planes have only one propeller. From two to four people can ride in the plane. Bigger propeller planes have two engines. They have a propeller under each wing. They can carry about twenty passengers on short trips.

Cargo Planes

A big airplane is waiting to take off. It is a cargo plane.

A cargo plane does not have seats. Instead, there is a big space inside the plane. This space carries goods and packages. Huge military cargo planes can carry tanks and trucks.

Takeoff

The pilot says, "We've been cleared for takeoff." Here we go!

The plane goes faster and faster down the runway. Then the wheels leave the ground. The plane goes up into the air. You are flying. The wings rushing through the air hold the plane up.

The First Planes

The first successful airplane was built by two brothers. Their names were Orville and Wilbur Wright. They flew their plane for the first time in 1903. The flight was near Kitty Hawk, North Carolina.

Soon, people were making and flying planes for fun. Then they made planes to use in war.

War Planes

The first war planes were small. They had propellers. They could not fly very far or go very fast. War planes are called military planes. Most military planes today are jets. Some war planes drop bombs. Fighter jets fight other war planes.

Special Kinds of Planes

Some airplanes do special jobs. Crop dusters spray farm fields to kill bugs or weeds.

Seaplanes do not need airports or runways. They can land on water.

Ultralights are very small planes. Many people fly ultralights for fun.

Bigger, Faster Planes

What will airplanes be like in the future? They will be bigger. They will also travel faster.

One day, you might fly in a plane with 600 other people. You might fly around the world in just a few hours. You might fly to the very edge of space!

Coming in for a Landing

This plane trip is almost over. It is time to land.

Air-traffic controllers tell the pilots when to land and which runway to use. Air-traffic controllers use special computer screens to watch every plane.

Look out the window and see the ground coming closer. Bump! The plane touches down on the runway. You have landed safely. This trip is over. Would you like to fly again?

Glossary

cargo—goods carried in a ship, an aircraft, or a vehicle

cockpit—the area in the front of a plane where the pilot sits

flight engineer—a member of an airplane crew who is responsible for the plane's mechanical operation

jet engine—motors powered by a stream of gases. These gases are made by burning a mixture of fuel and air inside the engine.

paved—covered with concrete or asphalt

propeller—a set of rotating blades that provide enough force to move a vehicle

Did You Know?

Orville and Wilbur Wright made their first flight on December 17, 1903.

The first nonstop flight from New York to Paris was made by Charles Lindbergh on May 21, 1927.

The United States is home to about 700,000 pilots.

The Concorde jet was introduced in 1976. It could fly at 1,350 miles (2,172 kilometers) per hour. It is the fastest passenger jet ever.

In 1932, Amelia Earhart became the first woman to fly alone across the Atlantic Ocean.

Want to Know More?

At the Library

Graham, Ian, and Tom Connell. *Aircraft: Built for Speed*. Austin, Tex.: Raintree Steck-Vaughn, 1998.

Hansen, Ole Steen. *20th Century Inventions: Aircraft*. Austin, Tex.: Raintree Steck-Vaughn, 1997.

Schaefer, Lola M. *Airplanes*. Mankato, Minn.: Bridgestone Books, 1999.

On the Web

Canadian Air Force—Snow Bird Squadron
http://www.snowbirds.dnd.ca/mmedia_e.asp
To learn about this group of Canadian military jet fliers

Wright Flyer Online
http://quest.arc.nasa.gov/aero/wright/
To explore a site devoted to the Wright Flyer Project

National Air and Space Museum
http://www.nasm.edu/galleries/gal109/NEWHTF/HTF500.HTM
To learn how and why planes fly

Planes of Fame

http://www.planesoffame.org

For a museum site with good photos of old planes

Kool Paper Airplanes

http://www.koolpaperairplanes.hypermart.net/index.htm

To learn how to fold and fly paper airplanes

Through the Mail

The American Institute of Aeronautics and Astronautics

Suite 500

1801 Alexander Bell Drive

Reston, VA 20191

On the Road

Smithsonian National Air and Space Museum

Seventh and Independence Avenue, S.W.

Washington, DC 20560

202/357-1400

Index

About the Author

Darlene R. Stille is a science editor and writer. She has lived in Chicago, Illinois, all her life. When she was in high school, she fell in love with science. While attending the University of Illinois, she discovered that she also enjoyed writing. Today she feels fortunate to have a career that allows her to pursue both her interests. Darlene R. Stille has written more than thirty books for young people.